AMORETTI

AMORETTI

WRITTEN NOT LONG SINCE
BY
EDMUNDE SPENSER

GYAN

Published by

Gyan Publishing House
5, Ansari Road
Daryaganj, New Delhi-110002
Phone: 011-47034999, 9811692060
E-mail: books@gyanbooks.com

Distribution Network
gyanbooks.com
India, USA, Canada, UK, Australia

ISBN: 978-93-6208-241-1 (PB)
First Published, 1595

2nd Impression 2024

Printed at: Gyan Press, Delhi.

AMORETTI
Author: EDMUNDE SPENSER

AMORETTI

WRITTEN NOT LONG SINCE

BY

EDMUNDE SPENSER

NEW YORK
THE LAUREL PRESS
MCMI

AMORETTI

HAPPY, ye leaves! when as those lilly hands,
Which hold my life in their dead-doing might,
Shall handle you, and hold in loves soft bands,
Lyke captives trembling at the victors sight.
And happy lines! on which, with starry light,
Those lamping eyes will deigne sometimes to look,
And reade the sorrowes of my dying spright,
Written with teares in harts close-bleeding book.
And happy rymes! bath'd in the sacred brooke
Of Helicon, whence she derived is;
When ye behold that Angels blessed looke,
My soules long-lacked foode, my heavens blis;
Leaves, lines, and rymes, seeke her to please alone,
Whom if ye please, I care for other none!

UNQUIET thought! whom at the first I bred
Of th' inward bale of my love-pined hart;
And sithens have with sighes and sorrowes fed,
Till greater then my wombe thou woxen art:
Breake forth at length out of the inner part,
In which thou lurkest lyke to vipers brood;
And seeke some succour both to ease my smart,
And also to sustayne thy selfe with food.
But, if in presence of that fayrest proud
Thou chance to come, fall lowly at her feet;
And, with meeke humblesse and afflicted mood,
Pardon for thee, and grace for me, intreat:
Which, if she graunt, then live, and my love cherish:
If not, die soone; and I with thee will perish.

THE soverayne beauty which I doo admyre,
Witnesse the world how worthy to be prayzed!
The light whereof hath kindled heavenly fyre
In my fraile spirit, by her from baseness raysed;
That, being now with her huge brightnesse dazed,
Base thing I can no more endure to view:
But, looking still on her, I stand amazed
At wondrous sight of so celestiall hew.
So when my toung would speak her praises dew,
It stopped is with thoughts astonishment;
And, when my pen would write her titles true,
It ravisht is with fancies wonderment:
Yet in my hart I then both speake and write
The wonder that my wit cannot endite.

NEW yeare, forth looking out of Janus gate,
Doth seeme to promise hope of new delight:
And, bidding th' old Adieu, his passed date
Bids all old thoughts to die in dumpish spright:
And, calling forth out of sad Winters night
Fresh Love, that long hath slept in cheerlesse bower,
Wils him awake, and soone about him dight
His wanton wings and darts of deadly power.
For lusty Spring now in his timely howre
Is ready to come forth, him to receive;
And warnes the Earth with divers-colord flowre
To decke hir selfe, and her faire mantle weave.
Then you, faire flowre! in whom fresh youth doth raine,
Prepare your selfe new love to entertaine.

RUDELY thou wrongest my deare harts desire,
In finding fault with her too portly pride:
The thing which I doo most in her admire,
Is of the world unworthy most envide:
For in those lofty lookes is close implide,
Scorn of base things, and sdeigne of foul dishonor:
Thretning rash eies which gaze on her so wide,
That loosely they ne dare to looke upon her.
Such pride is praise; such portlinesse is honor;
That boldned innocence beares in hir eies;
And her faire countenance, like a goodly banner,
Spreds in defiaunce of all enemies.
Was never in this world ought worthy tride,
Without some spark of such self-pleasing pride.

BE nought dismayd that her unmoved mind
Doth still persist in her rebellious pride:
Such love, not lyke to lusts of baser kynd,
The harder wonne, the firmer will abide.
The durefull Oake, whose sap is not yet dride,
Is long ere it conceive the kindling fyre;
But, when it once doth burne, it doth divide
Great heat, and makes his flames to heaven aspire.
So hard it is to kindle new desire
In gentle brest, that shall endure for ever:
Deepe is the wound, that dints the parts entire
With chast affects that naught but death can sever;
Then thinke not long in taking litle paine
To knit the knot, that ever shall remaine.

FAYRE eyes! the myrrour of my mazed hart,
What wondrous vertue is contaynd in you,
The which both lyfe and death forth from you dart,
Into the object of your mighty view?
For, when ye mildly looke with lovely hew,
Then is my soule with life and love inspired:
But when ye lowre, or looke on me askew,
Then doe I die, as one with lightning fyred.
But, since that lyfe is more then death desyred,
Looke ever lovely, as becomes you best;
That your bright beams, of my weak eies admyred,
May kindle living fire within my brest.
Such life should be the honor of your light,
Such death the sad ensample of your might.

MORE then most faire, full of the living fire,
Kindled above unto the Maker neere;
No eies but joyes, in which al powers conspire,
That to the world naught else be counted deare;
Thrugh your bright beams doth not the blinded guest
Shoot out his darts to base affections wound;
But Angels come to lead fraile mindes to rest
In chast desires, on heavenly beauty bound.
You frame my thoughts, and fashion me within;
You stop my toung, and teach my hart to speake;
You calme the storme that passion did begin,
Strong thrugh your cause, but by your vertue weak.
Dark is the world, where your light shined never;
Well is he borne, that may behold you ever.

LONG-WHILE I sought to what I might compare
Those powrefull eies, which lighten my dark spright;
Yet find I nought on earth, to which I dare
Resemble th' ymage of their goodly light.
Not to the Sun; for they doo shine by night;
Nor to the Moone; for they are changed never;
Nor to the Starres; for they have purer sight;
Nor to the Fire; for they consume not ever;
Nor to the Lightning; for they still persever;
Nor to the Diamond; for they are more tender;
Nor unto Cristall; for nought may them sever;
Nor unto Glasse; such baseness mought offend her.
Then to the Maker selfe they likest be,
Whose light doth lighten all that here we see.

UNRIGHTEOUS Lord of
Love, what law is this,
That me thou makest thus
tormented be,
The whiles she lordeth in li-
centious blisse
Of her freewill, scorning both
thee and me?
See! how the Tyrannesse doth joy to see
The huge massácres which her eyes do make;
And humbled harts brings captive unto thee,
That thou of them mayst mightie vengeance
take,
But her proud hart doe thou a little shake,
And that high look, with which she doth comp-
troll
All this world's pride, bow to a baser make,
And al her faults in thy black booke enroll:
That I may laugh at her in equall sort,
As she doth laugh at me, and makes my pain
her sport.

DAYLY when I do seeke and sew for peace,
And hostages doe offer for my truth;
She, cruell warriour, doth herselfe addresse
To battell, and the weary war renew'th;
Ne wilbe moov'd with reason, or with rewth,
To graunt small respit to my restlesse toile;
But greedily her fell intent poursewth,
Of my poore life to make unpittied spoile.
Yet my poore life, all sorrowes to assoyle,
I would her yield, her wrath to pacify:
But then she seeks, with torment and turmoyle,
To force me live, and will not let me dy.
All paine hath end, and every war hath peace;
But mine, no price nor prayer may surcease.

ONE day I sought with her hart-thrilling eies
To make a truce, and termes to entertaine:
All fearelesse then of so false enimies,
Which sought me to entrap in treasons traine.
So, as I then disarmed did remaine,
A wicked ambush which lay hidden long
In the close covert of her guilefull eyen,
Thence breaking forth, did thick about me throng,
Too feeble I t'abide the brunt so strong,
Was forst to yeeld my selfe into their hands;
Who, me captiving streight with rigorous wrong,
Have ever since me kept in cruell bands.
So, Ladie, now to you I doo complaine,
Against your eies, that justice I may gaine.

IN that proud port, which her so goodly graceth,
Whiles her faire face she reares up to the skie,
And to the ground her eie-lids low embaseth,
Most goodly temperature ye may descry;
Myld humblesse, mixt with awfull majesty.
For, looking on the earth whence she was borne,
Her minde remembreth her mortalitie,
Whatso is fayrest shall to earth returne.
But that same lofty countenance seemes to scorne
Base thing, and thinke how she to heaven may clime;
Treading downe earth as lothsome and forlorne,
That hinders heavenly thoughts with drossy slime.
Yet lowly still vouchsafe to looke on me;
Such lowlinesse shall make you lofty be.

RETOURNE agayne, my forces
late dismayd,
Unto the siege by you abandon'd quite.
Great shame it is to leave, like
one afrayd,
So fayre a peece, for one repulse so light,
Gaynst such strong castles needeth greater
might
Then those small forts which ye were wont
belay:
Such haughty mynds, enur'd to hardy fight,
Disdayne to yield unto the first assay.
Bring therefore all the forces that ye may,
And lay incessant battery to her heart;
Playnts, prayers, vowes, ruth, sorrow, and dismay;
Those engins can the proudest love convert:
And, if those fayle, fall downe and dy before
her;
So dying live, and living do adore her.

YE tradefull Merchants, that, with weary toyle,
Do seeke most pretious things to make your gain;
And both the Indias of their treasure spoile;
What needeth you to seeke so farre in vaine?
For loe, my love doth in her selfe containe
All this worlds riches that may farre be found:
If Saphyres, loe, her eies be Saphyres plaine;
If Rubies, loe, hir lips be Rubies sound;
If Pearles, hir teeth be Pearles, both pure and round;
If Yvorie, her forehead Yvory weene;
If Gold, her locks are finest Gold on ground;
If Silver, her faire hands are Silver sheene:
But that which fairest is, but few behold,
Her mind adornd with vertues manifold.

XV

ONE day as I unwarily did gaze
On those fayre eyes, my loves
immortall light;
The whiles my stonisht hart
stood in amaze,
Through sweet illusion of her
lookes delight;
I mote perceive how, in her
glauncing sight,
Legions of loves with little wings did fly;
Darting their deadly arrowes, fyry bright,
At every rash beholder passing by.
One of those archers closely I did spy,
Ayming his arrow at my very hart:
When suddenly, with twincle of her eye,
The Damzell broke his misintended dart.
Had she not so doon, sure I had bene slayne;
Yet as it was, I hardly scap't with paine.

THE glorious pourtraict of that Angels face,
Made to amaze weake mens confused skil,
And this worlds worthlesse glory to embase,
What pen, what pencill, can expresse her fill?
For though he colours could devize at will,
And eke his learned hand at pleasure guide,
Least, trembling, it his workmanship should spill;
Yet many wondrous things there are beside:
The sweet eye-glaunces, that like arrowes glide;
The charming smiles, that rob sence from the hart;
The lovely pleasance; and the lofty pride;
Cannot expressed be by any art.
A greater craftesmans hand thereto doth neede,
That can expresse the life of things indeed.

xvii

THE rolling wheele that runneth often round,
The hardest steele, in tract of time doth teare:
And drizling drops, that often doe redound,
The firmest flint doth in continuance weare:
Yet cannot I, with many a dropping teare
And long intreaty, soften her hard hart;
That she will once vouchsafe my plaint to heare,
Or looke with pitty on my payneful smart;
But, when I pleade, she bids me play my part;
And, when I weep, she sayes, Teares are but water,
And, when I sigh, she sayes, I know the art;
And, when I waile, she turnes hir selfe to laughter.
So do I weepe, and wayle, and pleade in vaine,
Whiles she as steele and flint doth still remayne.

THE merry Cuckow, messenger of Spring,
His trompet shrill hath thrise already sounded,
That warnes al lovers wayt upon their king,
Who now is comming forth with girland crouned.
With noyse whereof the quyre of Byrds resounded,
Their anthemes sweet, devized of loves prayse,
That all the woods theyr ecchoes back rebounded,
As if they knew the meaning of their layes.
But mongst them all, which did Loves honor rayse,
No word was heard of her that most it ought;
But she his precept proudly disobayes,
And doth his ydle message set at nought.
Therefore, O Love, unless she turne to thee
Ere Cuckow end, let her a rebell be!

IN vaine I seeke and sew to her for grace,
And doe myne humbled hart before her poure;
The whiles her foot she in my necke doth place,
And tread my life downe in the lowly floure.
And yet the Lyon that is Lord of power,
And reigneth over every beast in field,
In his most pride disdeigneth to devoure
The silly lambe that to his might doth yield.
But she, more cruell, and more salvage wylde,
Then either Lyon or the Lyonesse;
Shames not to be with guiltlesse bloud defylde,
But taketh glory in her cruelnesse.
Fayrer then fayrest! let none ever say,
That ye were blooded in a yeelded pray.

WAS it the worke of Nature or of Art,
Which tempred so the feature of her face,
That pride and meeknesse, mixt by equall part,
Doe both appeare t' adorne her beauties grace?
For with mild pleasance, which doth pride displace,
She to her love doth lookers eyes allure;
And, with sterne countenance, back again doth chace
Their looser lookes that stir up lustes impure;
With such strange termes her eyes she doth inure,
That, with one looke, she doth my life dismay;
And with another doth it streight recure;
Her smile me drawes; her frowne me drives away.
  Thus doth she traine and teach me with her lookes;
  Such art of eyes I never read in bookes!

THIS holy season, fit to fast and pray,
Men to devotion ought to be inclynd;
Therefore, I lykewise, on so holy day,
For my sweet Saynt some service fit will find.
Her temple fayre is built within my mind,
In which her glorious ymage placed is;
On which my thoughts doo day and night attend,
Lyke sacred priests that never thinke amisse!
There I to her, as th' author of my blisse,
Will builde an altar to appease her yre;
And on the same my hart will sacrifise,
Burning in flames of pure and chast desyre:
The which vouchsafe, O goddesse, to accept,
Amongst thy deerest relicks to be kept.

PENELOPE, for her Ulisses sake,
Deviz'd a Web her wooers to deceave;
In which the worke that she all day did make,
The same at night she did againe unreave:
Such subtile craft my Damzell doth conceave,
Th' importune suit of my desire to shonne:
For all that I in many dayes doo weave,
In one short houre I find by her undonne.
So, when I thinke to end that I begonne,
I must begin and never bring to end:
For with one looke she spils that long I sponne;
And with one word my whole years work doth rend.
Such labour like the Spyders web I fynd,
Whose fruitlesse worke is broken with least wynd.

WHEN I behold that beauties wonderment,
And rare perfection of each goodly part;
Of natures skill the onely complement;
I honor and admire the Makers art.
But when I feele the bitter balefull smart,
Which her fayre eyes unwares doe worke in mee,
That death out of theyr shiny beames doe dart;
I thinke that I a new Pandora see,
Whom all the Gods in councell did agree
Into this sinfull world from heaven to send;
That she to wicked men a scourge should bee,
For all their faults with which they did offend.
  But, since ye are my scourge, I will intreat,
  That for my faults ye will me gently beat.

HOW long shall this lyke dying lyfe endure,
And know no end of her owne mysery,
But wast and weare away in termes unsure,
Twixt feare and hope depending doubtfully!
Yet better were attonce to let me die,
And shew the last ensample of your pride;
Then to torment me thus with cruelty,
To prove your powre, which I too well have tride.
But yet if in your hardned brest ye hide
A close intent at last to shew me grace;
Then all the woes and wrecks which I abide,
As meanes of blisse I gladly wil embrace;
And wish that more and greater they might be,
That greater meede at last may turne to mee.

XXV

SWEET is the Rose, but growes upon a brere;
Sweet is the Junipere, but sharpe his bough;
Sweet is the Eglantine, but pricketh nere;
Sweet is the Firbloome, but his braunche is rough;
Sweet is the Cypresse, but his rynd is tough;
Sweet is the Nut, but bitter is his pill;
Sweet is the Broome-flowre, but yet sowre enough;
And sweet is Moly, but his root is ill.
So every sweet with soure is tempred still,
That maketh it be coveted the more:
For easie things, that may be got at will,
Most sorts of men doe set but little store.
Why then should I accoumpt of little paine.
That endlesse pleasure shall unto me gaine!

FAIRE Proud! now tell me, why should faire be proud,
Sith all worlds glorie is but drosse uncleane,
And in the shade of death it selfe shall shroud,
However now thereof ye little weene!
That goodly Idoll, now so gay beseene,
Shall doffe her fleshes borrowd fayre attyre,
And be forgot as it had never beene;
That many now much worship and admire!
Ne any then shall after it inquire,
Ne any mention shall thereof remaine,
But what this verse, that never shall expyre,
Shall to your purchas with her thankles paine!
Faire! be no lenger proud of that shall perish!
But that, which shall you make immortall cherish.

THE laurel-leafe, which you
this day doe weare,
Gives me great hope of your
relenting mynd:
For since it is the badge which
I doe beare,
Ye, bearing it, doe seeme to me
inclind:
The powre thereof, which ofte in me I find,
Let it lykewise your gentle brest inspire
With sweet infusion, and put you in mind
Of that proud mayd, whom now those leaves
attyre:
Proud Daphne, scorning Phœbus lovely fyre,
On the Thessalian shore from him did flie:
For which the gods, in theyr revengefull yre,
Did her transforme into a laurell-tree.
Then fly no more, fayre Love, from Phebus
chace,
But in your brest his leafe and love embrace.

SEE! how the stubborne damzell doth deprave
My simple meaning with disdaynfull scorne;
And by the bay, which I unto her gave,
Accoumpts my self her captive quite forlorne.
The bay (quoth she) is of the victours borne,
Yielded them by the vanquisht as theyr meeds,
And they therewith doe Poetes heads adorne,
To sing the glory of their famous deedes.
But sith she will the conquest challeng needs,
Let her accept me as her faithfull thrall:
That her great triumph, which my skill exceeds,
I may in trump of fame blaze over-all.
  Then would I decke her head with glorious bayes,
  And fill the world with her victorious prayse.

MY love is lyke to yse, and I to fyre;
How comes it then that this her cold so great
Is not dissolv'd through my so hot desyre,
But harder growes the more I her intreat!
Or how comes it that my exceeding heat
Is not delayd by her hart-frosen cold;
But that I burne much more in boyling sweat,
And feele my flames augmented manifold!
What more miraculous thing may be told,
That fire, which all things melts, should harden yse;
And yse, which is congeald with sencelesse cold,
Should kindle fyre by wonderfull devyse!
Such is the powre of love in gentle mind,
That it can alter all the course of kynd.

AH! why hath nature to so hard a hart
Given so goodly giftes of beauties grace!
Whose pryde depraves each other better part,
And all those pretious ornaments deface.
Sith to all other beastes of bloody race
A dreadfull countenaunce she given hath;
That with theyr terrour al the rest may chace,
And warne to shun the daunger of theyr wrath.
But my proud one doth worke the greater scath,
Through sweet allurement of her lovely hew;
That she the better may in bloody bath
Of such poor thralls her cruell hands embrew.
　But, did she know how ill these two accord,
　Such cruelty she would have soone abhord.

THE paynefull smith, with force of fervent heat,
The hardest yron soone doth mollify;
That with his heavy sledge he can it beat,
And fashion to what he it list apply.
Yet cannot all these flames, in which I fry,
Her hart more harde then yron soft a whit:
Ne all the playnts and prayers, with which I
Doe beat on th' andvile of her stubberne wit
But still, the more she fervent sees my fit,
The more she frieseth in her wilfull pryde;
And harder growes, the harder she is smit
With all the playnts which to her be applyde.
What then remaines but I to ashes burne,
And she to stones at length all frosen turne!

GREAT wrong I doe, I can it not deny,
To that most sacred Empresse, my dear dred,
Not finishing her Queene of Faëry,
That mote enlarge her living prayses, dead.
But Lodwick, this of grace to me aread;
Do ye not thinck th' accomplishment of it
Sufficient worke for one mans simple head,
All were it, as the rest, but rudely writ?
How then should I, without another wit,
Thinck ever to endure so tædious toyle!
Sins that this one is tost with troublous fit
Of a proud love, that doth my spirite spoyle.
  Ceasse then, till she vouchsafe to grawnt me rest;
  Or lend you me another living brest.

LYKE as a ship, that through the Ocean wyde,
By conduct of some star, doth make her way;
Whenas a storme hath dimd her trusty guyde,
Out of her course doth wander far astray!
So I, whose star, that wont with her bright ray
Me to direct, with cloudes is over-cast,
Doe wander now, in darknesse and dismay,
Through hidden perils round about me plast;
Yet hope I well that, when this storm is past,
My Helice, the lodestar of my lyfe,
Will shine again, and looke on me at last,
With lovely light to cleare my cloudy grief,
  Till then I wander carefull, comfortlesse,
  In secret sorow, and sad pensivenesse.

MY hungry eyes, through greedy covetize
Still to behold the object of their paine,
With no contentment can themselves suffize;
But, having, pine; and, having not, complaine.
For, lacking it, they cannot lyfe sustayne;
And, having it, they gaze on it the more;
In their amazement lyke Narcissus vaine,
Whose eyes him starv'd: so plenty makes me poore.
Yet are mine eyes so filled with the store
Of that faire sight, that nothing else they brooke,
But lothe the things which they did like before,
And can no more endure on them to looke.
All this worlds glory seemeth vayne to me,
And all their showes but shadowes, saving she.

TELL me, when shall these wearie woes have end,
Or shall their ruthlesse torment never cease;
But al my dayes in pining langour spend,
Without hope of aswagement or release?
Is there no meanes for me to purchace peace.
Or make agreement with her thrilling eyes;
But that their cruelty doth still increace,
And dayly more augment my miseryes?
But, when ye have shewd all extremityes,
Then thinke how litle glory ye have gayned
By slaying him, whose life, though ye despyse,
Mote have your life in honour long maintayned.
But by his death, which some perhaps will mone,
Ye shall condemned be of many a one.

WHAT guyle is this, that those her golden tresses
She doth attyre under a net of gold;
And with sly skill so cunningly them dresses,
That which is gold, or heare, may scarse be told?
Is it that mens frayle eyes, which gaze too bold,
She may entangle in that golden snare;
And, being caught, may craftily enfold
Theyr weaker harts, which are not wel aware?
Take heed, therefore, myne eyes, how ye doe stare
Henceforth too rashly on that guilefull net,
In which, if ever ye entrapped are,
Out of her bands ye by no meanes shall get.
Fondnesse it were for any, being free,
To covet fetters, though they golden bee!

ARION, when, through tempests cruel wracke,
He forth was thrown into the greedy seas;
Through the sweet musick, which his harp did make,
Allur'd a Dolphin him from death to ease.
But my rude musick, which was wont to please
Some dainty eares, cannot, with any skill,
The dreadfull tempest of her wrath appease,
Nor move the Dolphin from her stubborn will,
But in her pride she dooth persever still.
All carelesse how my life for her decayes:
Yet with one word she can it save or spill.
To spill were pitty, but to save were prayse!
Chose rather to be praysd for dooing good,
Then to be blam'd for spilling guiltlesse blood.

SWEET Smile! the daughter of the Quęene of Love,
Expressing all thy mothers powrefull art.
With which she wants to temper angry Jove,
When all the gods he threats with thundring dart:
Sweet is thy vertue, as thy selfe sweet art.
For, when on me thou shinedst late in sadnesse,
A melting pleasance ran through every part,
And me revived with hart-robbing gladnesse.
Whylest rapt with joy resembling heavenly madnes,
My soule was ravisht quite as in a traunce;
And feeling thence, no more her sorowes sadnesse,
Fed on the fulnesse of that chearefull glaunce.
More sweet than Nectar, or Ambrosiall meat,
Seemd every bit which thenceforth I did eat.

MARK when she smiles with amiable cheare,
And tell me whereto can ye lyken it;
When on each eyelid sweetly doe appeare
An hundred Graces as in shade to sit.
Lykest it seemeth, in my simple wit,
Unto the fayre sunshine in somers day;
That, when a dreadfull storme away is flit,
Thrugh the broad world doth spred his goodly ray;
At sight whereof, each bird that sits on spray,
And every beast that to his den was fled,
Comes forth afresh out of their late dismay,
And to the light lift up theyr drouping hed.
So my storme-beaten hart likewise is cheared
With that sunshine, when cloudy looks are cleared.

IS it her nature, or is it her will,
To be so cruell to an humbled foe?
If nature; then she may it mend with skill:
If will; then she at will may will forgoe.
But if her nature and her wil be so,
That she will plague the man that loves her most,
And take delight t' encrease a wretches woe;
Then all her natures goodly guifts are lost:
And that same glorious beauties ydle boast
Is but a bayt such wretches to beguile,
As, being long in her loves tempest tost,
She meanes at last to make her pitious spoyle.
O fayrest fayre! let never it be named,
That so fayre beauty was so fowly shamed.

THE love which me so cruelly tormenteth,
So pleasing is in my extreamest paine,
That, all the more my sorrow it augmenteth,
The more I love and doe embrace my bane.
Ne doe I wish (for wishing were but vaine)
To be acquit fro my continual smart;
But joy, her thrall for ever to remayne,
And yield for pledge my poor captyvëd hart;
The which, that it from her may never start,
Let her, yf please her, bynd with adamant chayne:
And from all wandring loves, which mote pervart
His safe assurance, strongly it restrayne.
Onely let her abstaine from cruelty.
And doe me not before my time to dy.

SHALL I then silent be, or shall I speake?
And, if I speake, her wrath renew I shall;
And, if I silent be, my hart will breake,
Or choked be with overflowing gall.
What tyranny is this, both my hart to thrall,
And eke my toung with proud restraint to tie;
That nether I may speake nor thinke at all,
But like a stupid stock in silence die!
Yet I my hart with silence secretly
Will teach to speak, and my just cause to plead;
And eke mine eies, with meek humility,
Love-learned letters to her eyes to read;
Which her deep wit, that true harts thought can spel,
Wil soon conceive, and learne to construe well.

WHEN those renoumed noble
Peres of Greece,
Thrugh stubborn pride,
amongst themselves did jar,
Forgetfull of the famous gold-
en fleece;
Then Orpheus with his harp
theyr strife did bar.
But this continuall, cruell, civill warre,
The which my selfe against my selfe doe make;
Whilest my weak powres of passions warreid
arre;
No skill can stint, nor reason can aslake.
But, when in hand my tuneleese harp I take,
Then doe I more augment my foes despight;
And griefe renew, and passions doe awake
To battaile, fresh against my selfe to fight.
Mongst whome the more I seeke to settle
peace.
The more I fynd their malice to increase.

LEAVE, lady! in your glasse of cristall clene,
Your goodly selfe for evermore to vew:
And in my selfe, my inward selfe, I meane,
Most lively lyke behold your semblant trew.
Within my hart, though hardly it can shew
Thing so divine to vew of earthly eye,
The fayre Idea of your celestiall hew
And every part remaines immortally:
And were it not that, through your cruelty,
With sorrow dimmed and deform'd it were,
The goodly ymage of your visnomy,
Clearer then cristall, would therein appere.
  But, if your selfe in me ye playne will see,
  Remove the cause by which your fayre beames darkned be.

WHEN my abodes prefixed time is spent,
My cruell fayre streight bids me wend my way:
But then from heaven most hideous stormes are sent,
As willing me against her will to stay.
Whom then shall I, or heaven or her, obay?
The heavens know best what is the best for me:
But as she will, whose will my life doth sway,
My lower heaven, so it perforce must bee.
But ye high hevens, that all this sorowe see,
Sith all your tempests cannot hold me backe,
Aswage your storms; or else both you, and she,
Will both together me too sorely wracke.
  Enough it is for one man to sustaine
  The stormes, which she alone on me doth raine.

TRUST not the treason of those smyling lookes,
Untill ye have theyr guylefull traynes well tryde:
For they are lyke but unto golden hookes,
That from the foolish fish theyr bayts doe hyde:
So she with flattring smyles weake harts doth guyde
Unto her love, and tempte to theyr decay;
Whome, being caught, she kills with cruell pryde,
And feeds at pleasure on the wretched pray:
Yet, even whylst her bloody hands them slay,
Her eyes looke lovely, and upon them smyle;
That they take pleasure in her cruell play,
And, dying, doe themselves of payne beguyle.
O mighty charm! which makes men love theyr bane,
And thinck they dy with pleasure, live with payne.

INNOCENT paper; whom too cruell hand
Did make the matter to avenge her yre:
And, ere she could thy cause wel understand,
Did sacrifize unto the greedy fyre.
Well worthy thou to have found better hyre,
Then so bad end for hereticks ordayned;
Yet heresy nor treason didst conspire,
But plead thy maisters cause, unjustly payned.
Whom she, all carelesse of his griefe constrayned
To utter forth the anguish of his hart:
And would not heare, when he to her complayned
The piteous passion of his dying smart.
Yet live for ever, though against her will,
And speake her good, though she requite it ill.

FAYRE cruell! why are ye so fierce and cruell?
Is it because your eyes have powre to kill?
Then know that mercy is the Mighties jewell:
And greater glory thinke, to save then spill.
But if it be your pleasure, and proud will,
To shew the powre of your imperious eyes;
Then not on him that never thought you ill,
But bend your force against your enemyes:
Let them feele the utmost of your crueltyes;
And kill with looks as Cockatrices doo:
But him, that at your footstoole humbled lies,
With mercifull regard give mercy too.
Such mercy shall you make admyr'd to be;
So shall you live, by giving life to me.

LONG languishing in double malady
Of my harts wound, and of my bodies griefe;
There came to me a leach, that would apply
Fit medicines for my bodies best reliefe.
Vayne man, quod I, that hast but little priefe
In deep discovery of the mynds disease;
Is not the hart of all the body chiefe,
And rules the members as it selfe doth please?
Then, with some cordialls, seeke first to appease
The inward languor of my wounded hart,
And then my body shall have shortly ease:
But such sweet cordialls passe Physitions art.
Then, my lyfes Leach! doe your skill reveale;
And, with one salve, both hart and body heale.

DOE I not see that fayrest ymages
Of hardest marble are of purpose made,
For that they should endure through many ages,
Ne let theyr famous moniments to fade?
Why then doe I, untrainde in lovers trade,
Her hardnes blame, which I should more commend?
Sith neve rought was excellent assayde
Which was not hard t' atchieve and bring to end.
Ne ought so hard, but he, that would attend,
Mote soften it and to his will allure:
So doe I hope her stubborne hart to bend,
And that it then more stedfast will endure:
Onely my paines wil be the more to get her,
But, having her, my joy wil be the greater.

SO oft as homeward I from her depart,
I goe lyke one that, having lost the field,
Is prisoner led away with heavy hart,
Despoyld of warlike armes and knowen shield.
So doe I now my selfe a prisoner yeeld
To sorrow and to solitary paine;
From presence of my dearest deare exylde,
Long-while alone in langour to remaine.
There let no thought of joy, or pleasure vaine,
Dare to approch, that may my solace breed;
But sudden dumps, and drery sad disdayne
Of all worlds gladnesse, more my torment feed.
  So I her absens will my penaunce make,
  That of her presens I my meed may take.

THE Panther, knowing that his spotted hyde
Doth please all beasts, but that his looks them fray;
Within a bush his dreadfull head doth hide,
To let them gaze, whylest he on them may pray:
Right so my cruell fayre with me doth play;
For, with the goodly semblant of her hew,
She doth allure me to mine owne decay,
And then no mercy will unto me shew.
Great shame it is, thing so divine in view,
Made for to be the worlds most ornament,
To make the bayte her gazers to embrew:
Good shames to be to ill an instrument!
But mercy doth with beautie best agree,
As in theyr Maker ye them best may see.

OF this worlds Theatre in which
we stay,
My love, lyke the Spectator,
ydly sits;
Beholding me, that all the
pageants play,
Disguysing diversly my troub-
led wits.
Sometimes I joy when glad occasion fits,
And mask in myrth lyke to a Comedy:
Soone after, when my joy to sorrow flits,
I waile, and make my woes a Tragedy.
Yet she, beholding me with constant eye,
Delights not in my merth, nor rues my smart:
But, when I laugh, she mocks; and, when I cry,
She laughes, and hardens evermore her hart.
What then can move her? if nor merth nor
mone,
She is no woman, but a sencelesse stone.

So oft as I her beauty doe behold,
And therewith doe her cruelty compare,
I marvaile of what substance was the mould,
The which her made attonce so cruell faire.
Not earth; for her high thoghts more heavenly are:
Not water; for her love doth burne like fyre:
Not ayre; for she is not so light or rare:
Not fyre; for she doth friese with faint desire.
Then needs another Element inquire
Whereof she mote be made, that is, the skye.
For to the heaven her haughty lookes aspire:
And eke her mind is pure immortall hye.
Then, sith so heaven ye lykened are the best,
Be lyke in mercy as in all the rest.

lv

FAYRE ye be sure, but cruell and unkind,
As is a Tygre, that with greedinesse
Hunts after bloud; when he by chance doth find
A feeble beast, doth felly him oppresse.
Fayre be ye sure, but proud and pittilesse,
As is a storme, that all things doth prostrate;
Finding a tree alone all comfortlesse,
Beats on it strongly, it to ruinate.
Fayre be ye sure, but hard and obstinate,
As is a rocke amidst the raging floods:
Gaynst which, a ship, of succour desolate,
Doth suffer wreck both of her selfe and goods.
That ship, that tree, and that same beast, am I,
Whom ye doe wreck, doe ruine, and destroy.

SWEET warriour! when shall I have peace with you?
High time it is this warre now ended were
Which I no lenger can endure to sue,
Ne your incessant battry more to beare:
So weake my powres, so sore my wounds, appeare,
That wonder is how I should live a jot,
Seeing my hart through-launced every where
With thousand arrowes, which your eies have shot:
Yet shoot ye sharpely still, and spare me not,
But glory thinke to make these cruel stoures.
Ye cruell one! what glory can be got,
In slaying him that would live gladly yours!
Make peace therefore, and graunt me timely grace,
That al my wounds wil heale in little space.

By her that is most assured to her selfe.

WEAKE is th' assurance that weake flesh reposeth
In her owne powre, and scorneth others ayde;
That soonest fals, when as she most supposeth
Her selfe assurd, and is of nought affrayd.
All flesh is frayle, and all her strength unstayd,
Like a vaine bubble blowen up with ayre:
Devouring tyme and changeful chance have prayd,
Her glories pride that none may it repayre.
Ne none so rich or wise, so strong or fayre,
But fayleth, trusting on his owne assurance;
And he, that standeth on the hyghest stayre,
Fals lowest; for on earth nought hath endurance.
Why then doe ye, proud fayre, misdeeme so farre,
That to your selfe ye most assured arre!

THRISE happie she! that is so well assured
Unto her selfe, and setled so in hart,
That nether will for better be allured,
Ne feard with worse to any chaunce to start;
But, like a steddy ship, doth strongly part
The raging waves, and keepes her course aright;
Ne ought for tempest doth from it depart,
Ne ought for fayrer weathers false delight.
Such selfe-assurance need not feare the spight
Of grudging foes, ne favour seek of friends:
But, in the stay of her owne stedfast might,
Nether to one her selfe nor other bends.
Most happy she, that most assur'd doth rest;
But he most happy, who such one loves best.

THEY, that in course of heavenly spheares are skild,
To every planet point his sundry yeare:
In which her circles voyage is fulfild,
As Mars in three-score yeares doth run his spheare.
So, since the winged god his planet cleare
Began in me to move, one yeare is spent:
The which doth longer unto me appeare,
Then al those fourty which my life out-went.
Then by that count, which lovers books invent,
The spheare of Cupid fourty yeares containes:
Which I have wasted in long languishment,
That seemd the longer for my greater paines.
But let my loves fayre Planet short her wayes,
This yeare ensuing, or else short my dayes.

THE glorious image of the Makers beautie,
My soverayne saynt, the Idoll of my thought,
Dare not henceforth, above the bounds of dewtie,
T' accuse of pride, or rashly blame for ought.
For being, as she is, divinely wrought,
And of the brood of Angels hevenly borne;
And with the crew of blessed Saynts upbrought,
Each of which did her with theyr guifts adorne;
The bud of joy, the blossome of the morne,
The beame of light, whom mortal eyes admyre;
What reason is it then but she should scorne
Base things, that to her love too bold aspire!
Such heavenly formes ought rather worshipt be,
Then dare be lov'd by men of meane degree.

THE weary yeare his race now having run,
The new begins his compast course anew:
With shew of morning mylde he hath begun,
Betokening peace and plenty to ensew.
So let us, which this chaunge of weather vew,
Chaunge eke our mynds, and former lives amend;
The old yeares sinnes forepast let us eschew,
And fly the faults with which we did offend.
Then shall the new yeares joy forth freshly send,
Into the glooming world, his gladsome ray:
And all these stormes, which now his beauty blend,
Shall turne to caulmes, and tymely cleare away.
So, likewise, Love! cheare you your heavy spright,
And chaunge old yeares annoy to new delight.

AFTER long stormes and tempests sad assay,
Which hardly I endured heretofore,
In dread of death, and daungerous dismay,
With which my silly barke was tossed sore:
I doe at length descry the happy shore,
In which I hope ere long for to arryve:
Fayre soyle it seemes from far, and fraught with store
Of all that deare and daynty is alyve.
Most happy he! that can at last atchyve
The joyous safety of so sweet a rest;
Whose least delight sufficeth to deprive
Remembrance of all paines which him opprest.
All paines are nothing in respect of this;
All sorrowes short that gaine eternall blisse.

COMMING to kisse her lyps, (such grace I found,)
Me seemd, I smelt a gardin of sweet flowres,
That dainty odours from them threw around,
For damzels fit to decke their lovers bowres.
Her lips did smell lyke unto Gillyflowers;
Her ruddy cheekes, lyke unto Roses red;
Her snowy browes, like budded Bellamoures;
Her lovely eyes, lyke Pincks but newly spred;
Her goodly bosome, lyke a Strawberry bed;
Her neck, lyke to a bounch of Cullambynes;
Her brest, lyke Lillyes, ere theyr leaves be shed;
Her nipples, lyke yong blossomed Jessemynes:
Such fragrant flowers doe give most odorous smell;
But her sweet odour did them all excell.

THE doubt which ye misdeeme, fayre love, is vaine,
That fondly feare to loose your liberty;
When, loosing one, two liberties ye gayne,
And make him bond that bondage earst dyd fly.
Sweet be the bands, the which true love doth tye
Without constraynt, or dread of any ill:
The gentle birde feeles no captivity
Within her cage; but singes, and feeds her fill.
There pride dare not approch, nor discord spill
The league twixt them, that loyal love hath bound:
But simple truth, and mutuall good-will,
Seekes with sweet peace, to salve each others wound:
There Fayth doth fearlesse dwell in brasen towre,
And spotlesse Pleasure builds her sacred bowre.

TO all those happy blessings which ye have
With plenteous hand by heaven upon you thrown;
This one disparagement they to you gave,
That ye your love lent to so meane a one.
Yee, whose high worths surpassing paragon
Could not on earth have found one fit for mate,
Ne but in heaven matchable to none,
Why did ye stoup unto so lowly state?
But ye thereby much greater glory gate,
Then had ye sorted with a princes pere:
For, now your light doth more itselfe dilate,
And, in my darknesse, greater doth appeare,
Yet, since your light hath once enlumind me,
With my reflex yours shall encreased be.

LYKE as a huntsman after weary chace,
Seeing the game from him escapt away,
Sits downe to rest him in some shady place,
With panting hounds beguiled of their pray:
So, after long pursuit and vaine assay,
When I all weary had the chace forsooke,
The gentle deare returnd the selfe-same way,
Thinking to quench her thirst at the next brooke:
There she, beholding me with mylder looke,
Sought not to fly, but fearlesse still did bide;
Till I in hand her yet halfe trembling tooke,
And with her owne goodwill hir fyrmely tyde.
Strange thing, me seemd, to see a beast so wyld,
So goodly wonne, with her owne will beguyld.

lxvii

MOST glorious Lord of lyfe! that, on this day,
Didst make thy triumph over death and sin;
And, having harrowd hell, didst bring away
Captivity thence captive, us to win:
This joyous day, deare Lord, with joy begin;
And grant that we, for whom thou diddest dye,
Being with thy deare blood clene washt from sin,
May live for ever in felicity!
And that thy love we weighing worthily,
May likewise love thee for the same againe;
And for thy sake, that all lyke deare didst buy,
With love may one another entertayne!
So let us love, deare love, lyke as we ought:
Love is the lesson which the Lord us taught.

lxviii

THE famous warriors of anticke world
Used Trophees to erect in stately wize;
In which they would the records have enrold
Of theyr great deeds and valorous emprize.
What trophee then shall I most fit devize,
In which I may record the memory
Of my loves conquest, peerelesse beauties prise,
Adorn'd with honour, love, and chastity!
Even this verse, vowd to eternity,
Shall be thereof immortall moniment;
And tell her prayse to all posterity,
That may admire such worlds rare wonderment;
The happy purchase of my glorious spoile,
Gotton at last with labour and long toyle.

FRESH Spring, the herald of loves mighty king,
In whose cote-armour richly are displayd
All sorts of flowers, the which on earth do spring,
In goodly colours gloriously arrayd;
Goe to my love, where she is carelesse layd,
Yet in her winters bowre not well awake;
Tell her the joyous time wil not be staid,
Unlesse she doe him by the forelock take;
Bid her therefore her selfe soone ready make,
To wayt on Love amongst his lovely crew;
Where every one, that misseth then her make,
Shall be by him amearst with penance dew,
  Make hast, therefore, sweet love, whilest it is prime;
  For none can call againe the passed time.

I JOY to see how, in your drawen work,
Your selfe unto the Bee ye doe compare;
And me unto the Sypder, that doth lurke
In close awayt, to catch her unaware:
Right so your selfe were caught in cunning snare
Of a deare foe, and thralled to his love;
In whose streight bands ye now captived are
So firmely, that ye never may remove.
But as your worke is woven all above
With woodbynd flowers and fragrant Eglantine;
So sweet your prison you in time shall prove,
With many deare delights bedecked fyne.
And all thensforth eternall peace shall see
Betweene the Spyder and the gentle Bee.

OFT, when my spirit doth spred her bolder winges,
In mind to mount up to the purest sky;
It down is weighd with thoght of earthly things,
And clogd with burden of mortality;
Where, when that soverayne beauty it doth spy,
Resembling heavens glory in her light,
Drawne with sweet pleasures bayt, it back doth fly,
And unto heaven forgets her former flight.
There my fraile fancy, fed with full delight,
Doth bath in blisse, and mantleth most at ease;
Ne thinks of other heaven, but how it might
Her harts desire with most contentment please.
Hart need not wish none other happinesse,
But here on earth to have such hevens blisse.

BEING my self captyved here in care,
My hart, (whom none with servile bands can tye,
But the fayre tresses of your golden hayre,)
Breaking his prison, forth to you doth fly.
Lyke as a byrd, that in ones hand doth spy
Desired food, to it doth make his flight:
Even so my hart, that wont on your fayre eye
To feed his fill, flyes backe unto your sight.
Doe you him take, and in your bosome bright
Gently encage, that he may be your thrall:
Perhaps he there may learne, with rare delight,
To sing your name and prayses over-all:
That it hereafter may you not repent,
Him lodging in your bosome to have lent.

MOST happy letters! fram'd by skilfull trade,
With which that happy name was first desynd,
The which three times thrise happy hath me made,
With guifts of body, fortune, and of mind.
The first my being to me gave by kind,
From mothers womb deriv'd by dew descent:
The second is my sovereigne Queene most kind,
That honour and large richesse to me lent:
The third, my love, my lifes last ornament,
By whom my spirit out of dust was raysed:
To speake her prayse and glory excellent,
Of all alive most worthy to be praysed.
Ye three Elizabeths! for ever live,
That three such graces did unto me give.

lxxiv

ONE day I wrote her name upon the strand;
But came the waves, and washed it away:
Agayne, I wrote it with a second hand;
But came the tyde; and made my paynes his pray.
Vayne man, sayd she, that doest in vaine assay
A mortall thing so to immortalize;
For I my selve shall lyke to this decay,
And eek my name bee wyped out lykewise.
Not so, quod I; let baser things devize
To dy in dust, but you shall live by fame:
My verse your vertues rare shall eternize,
And in the hevens wryte your glorious name.
    Where, whenas death shall all the world subdew,
    Our love shall live, and later life renew.

FAYRE bosome! fraught with vertues richest tresure,
The neast of love, the lodging of delight,
The bowre of blisse, the paradice of pleasure,
The sacred harbour of that hevenly spright;
How was I ravisht with your lovely sight,
And my frayle thoughts too rashly led astray!
Whiles diving deepe through amorous insight,
On the sweet spoyle of beautie they did pray;
And twixt her paps, (like early fruit in May,
Whose harvest seemd to hasten now apace,)
They loosely did theyr wanton winges display,
And there to rest themselves did boldly place.
Sweet thoughts! I envy your so happy rest,
Which oft I wisht, yet never was so blest.

WAS it a dreame, or did I see it playne;
A goodly table of pure yvory,
All spred with juncats, fit to entertayne
The greatest Prince with pompous roialty:
Mongst which, there in a silver dish did ly
Twoo golden apples of unvalewd price;
Far passing those which Hercules came by,
Or those which Atalanta did entice;
Exceeding sweet, yet voyd of sinfull vice;
That many sought, yet none could ever taste;
Sweet fruit of pleasure, brought from Paradice
By Love himselfe, and in his garden plaste.
Her brest that table was, so richly spredd;
My thoughts the guests, which would thereon have fedd.

LACKYNG my love, I go from place to place,
Lyke a young fawne, that late hath lost the hynd;
And seeke each where, where last I sawe her face,
Whose ymage yet I carry fresh in mynd.
I seeke the fields with her late footing synd;
I seeke her bowre with her late presence deckt;
Yet nor in field nor bowre I her can fynd;
Yet field and bowre are full of her aspect:
But, when myne eyes I thereunto direct,
They ydly back returne to me agayne:
And, when I hope to see theyr trew objéct,
I fynd my selfe but fed with fancies vayne.
Ceasse then, myne eyes, to seeke her selfe to see;
And let my thoughts behold her selfe in mee.

MEN call you fayre, and you doe credit it,
For that your selfe ye dayly such doe see:
But the trew fayre, that is the gentle wit,
And vertuous mind, is much more praysd of me:
For all the rest, how ever fayre it be,
Shall turne to nought and loose that glorious hew;
But onely that is permanent and free
From frayle corruption, that doth flesh ensew.
That is true beautie: that doth argue you
To be divine, and borne of heavenly seed;
Deriv'd from that fayre Spirit, from whom al true
And perfect beauty did at first proceed:
He onely fayre, and what he fayre hath made;
All other fayre, lyke flowres, untymely fade.

AFTER so long a race as I have run
Through Faery land, which those six books compile,
Give leave to rest me being halfe fordonne,
And gather to myselfe new breath awhile.
Then, as a steed refreshed after toyle,
Out of my prison I will breake anew;
And stoutly will that second worke assoyle,
With strong endevour and attention dew.
Till then give leave to me, in pleasant mew
To sport my muse, and sing my loves sweet praise;
The contemplation of whose heavenly hew,
My spirit to an higher pitch will rayse,
But let her prayses yet be low and meane,
Fit for the handmayd of the Faery Queene.

lxxx

FAYRE is my love, when her fayre golden heares
With the loose wynd ye waving chance to marke;
Fayre, when the rose in her red cheekes appeares;
Or in her eyes the fyre of love does sparke.
Fayre, when her brest, lyke a rich laden barke,
With pretious merchandize she forth doth lay;
Fayre, when that cloud of pryde, which oft doth dark
Her goodly light, with smiles she drives away.
But fayrest she, when so she doth display
The gate with pearles and rubyes richly dight;
Throgh which her words so wise do make their way
To beare the message of her gentle spright.
The rest be works of natures wonderment:
But this the worke of harts astonishment.

lxxxi

JOY of my life! full oft for loving you
I blesse my lot, that was so lucky placed:
But then the more your owne mishap I rew,
That are so much by so meane love embased.
For, had the equall hevens so much you graced
In this as in the rest, ye mote invent
Som hevenly wit, whose verse could have enchased
Your glorious name in golden moniment.
But since ye deignd so goodly to relent
To me your thrall, in whom is little worth;
That little, that I am, shall all be spent
In setting your immortall prayses forth:
Whose lofty argument, uplifting me,
Shall lift you up unto an high degree.

LET not one sparke of filthy lustfull fyre
Breake out, that may her sacred peace molest;
Ne one light glance of sensuall desyre
Attempt to work her gentle mindes unrest:
But pure affections bred in spotlesse brest,
And modest thoughts breathd from wel-tempred sprites,
Goe visit her in her chast bowre of rest
Accompanyde with angelick delightes.
There fill your selfe with those most joyous sights,
The which my selfe could never yet attayne:
But speake no word to her of these sad plights,
Which her too constant stiffenesse doth constrayn.
  Onely behold her rare perfection.
  And blesse your fortunes fayre election.

THE world that cannot deeme of worthy things,
When I doe praise her, say I doe but flatter:
So does the Cuckow, when the Mavis sings,
Begin his witlesse note apace to clatter.
But they that skill not of so heavenly matter,
All that they know not envy or admyre;
Rather then envy, let them wonder at her,
But not to deeme of her desert aspyre.
Deepe, in the closet of my parts entyre,
Her worth is written with a golden quill,
That me with heavenly fury doth inspire,
And my glad mouth with her sweet prayses fill.
Which when as Fame in her shrill trump shal thunder,
Let the world chose to envy or to wonder.

VENEMOUS toung, tipt with vile adders sting,
Of that selfe kynd with which the Furies fell
Theyr snaky heads doe combe, from which a spring
Of poysoned words and spitefull speeches well;
Let all the plagues, and horrid paines, of hell
Upon thee fall for thine accursed hyre
That with false forged lyes, which thou didst tel,
In my true love did stirre up coles of yre;
The sparkes whereof let kindle thine own fyre,
And, catching hold on thine owne wicked hed,
Consume thee quite, that didst with guile conspire
In my sweet peace such breaches to have bred!
Shame be thy meed, and mischiefe thy reward,
Dew to thy selfe, that it for me prepard!

SINCE I did leave the presence of my love,
Many long weary dayes I have outworne;
And many nights, that slowly seemd to move
Theyr sad protract from evening untill morne.
For, when as day the heaven doth adorne,
I wish that night the noyous day would end:
And, when as night hath us of light forlorne,
I wish that day would shortly reascend.
Thus I the time with expectation spend,
And faine my griefe with chaunges to beguile,
That further seemes his terme still to extend,
And maketh every minute seeme a myle.
So sorrow still doth seeme too long to last;
But joyous houres doe fly away too fast.

SINCE I have lackt the comfort of that light,
The which was wont to lead my thoughts astray;
I wander as in darkenesse of the night,
Affrayd of every dangers least dismay.
Ne ought I see, though in the clearest day,
When others gaze upon theyr shadowes vayne,
But th' onely image of that heavenly ray,
Whereof some glance doth in mine eie remayne.
Of which beholding the Idæa playne,
Through contemplation of my purest part,
With light thereof I doe my selfe sustayne,
And thereon feed my love-affamisht hart.
But, with such brightnesse whylest I fill my mind,
I starve my body, and mine eyes doe blynd.

LYKE as the Culver, on the bared bough,
Sits mourning for the absence of her mate;
And, in her songs, sends many a wishfull vow
For his returne that seemes to linger late:
So I alone, now left disconsolate,
Mourne to my selfe the absence of my love,
And, wandring here and there all desolate,
Seek with my playnts to match that mournful dove.
Ne joy of ought that under heaven doth hove
Can comfort me, but her owne joyous sight:
Whose sweet aspect both God and man can move,
In her unspotted pleasauns to delight.
Dark is my day, whyles her fayre light I mis,
And dead my life that wants such lively blis.